THROUGH A MOTHER'S EYES

Poems of Love, Loss and Moving Forward

Copyright © Jackie Barreau 2013

This book is copyright. Apart from any fair dealing for the purposes of private study, research, criticism or review, as permitted under the Copyright Act, no part may be reproduced by any process without written permission. Enquiries should be addressed to the publisher.

Title: Through a Mother's Eyes
Author: Jackie Barreau
Email:jackie_barreau@live.com.au
Twitter: www.twitter.com/luvhopecourage
Facebook : www.facebook.com/lovehopeandcourage
Blog: www.lovehopeandcourage.wordpress.com

Cataloguing-in-Publication Data
Available from the National Library of Australia

ISBN: 978-0-646-59425-5

First Published in Australia by Jackie Barreau 2013

Book layout and design by
Publicious Pty Ltd
www.publicious.com.au

Book cover design © Andrew Williams
Front cover image © iStockphoto.com | Amanda Rohde
Back cover image © SD Smart redbubble.com/people/smarti77
Back cover portrait photo © Debra Law
Photographic images © SD Smart redbubble.com/people/smarti77
Illustrations © Claudiu Badea | Dreamstime.com

Dedicated to our beautiful boys, Cody and Luke,
and to all the brave children who have earned their angel wings.

In Memory of _____

"The two hardest things to say in life are hello for the first time and goodbye for the last." – Moira Rogers

Preface

This book was borne out of inspiration for the many bereaved parents and their terminally ill children who receive treatment and support through the Paediatric Palliative Care Service at the Women's and Children's Hospital in Adelaide South Australia.

Some of these poems were written after the losses of our two sons, Cody Alan (stillborn at 26 weeks) in September 1998 and Luke James (Neuroblastoma) in December 1998, who both received care through the Women's and Children's Hospital, Adelaide.

Both boys passed away within three months of each other, and as our world seemed to fall apart, we took comfort from the support given to us from the Paediatric Palliative Care Service.
This was my way of dealing with the deaths of our two sons, through verse.

So much has happened in the last nine months or so, and truthfully the impetus or catalyst for writing this book came from our eldest daughter Tayla's diagnosis in March of 2012.

Her symptoms at times matched that of her elder brother and were, quite honestly, frightening. As parents you worry about your children growing up in today's society and just being accepted by their peers, hoping that you teach and instil in them love, compassion and respect for all human beings.

Never do you ever feel you will be faced with a dilemma as to how your children will handle an illness, and learn to accept it. But Tayla has handled this remarkably well considering the circumstances. I hope and pray every day that this will be different and that we won't ever have to walk that familiar path like we did some fourteen years ago.

These poems are very raw and honest, and sometimes exhibit dark undertones, as spiralling episodes of depression and a roller coaster of emotion threatens to consume.

But ultimately they do end with a positive message of love, hope and courage, qualities that bereaved parents all face on their journey.

Introduction

Luke James Barreau was born on the 8th of August 1996, and he was our first son. He was everything you would expect your first baby to be, healthy and happy. But at 13 months of age he was diagnosed with stage four Neuroblastoma, an aggressive malignant childhood cancer. This was in September of 1997, around the time the Adelaide Crows won their inaugural AFL Premiership.

During his treatment as an inpatient in The Brookman Ward at the Women's and Children's Hospital, Luke endured months of chemotherapy, an operation to remove his tumour some months later, further chemotherapy, a stem cell transplant, and finally radiotherapy at the RAH, Adelaide.

I fell pregnant while he underwent his treatment, and we were looking forward to expanding our family.

We now fast forward to early September of 1998, and it was whilst Luke was undergoing some routine tests at the hospital that I mentioned to the nurses that I hadn't felt the baby moving. An ultrasound was arranged and it was discovered that the baby had no heart beat.

So at 26 weeks' gestation, I suffered a stillbirth. Our precious but lifeless little baby was wrapped in a blanket and bonnet and we named him Cody Alan.

Then on the 20th of December 1998, our special little boy Luke, lost his brave battle with Neuroblastoma. He lasted just three weeks at home receiving palliative care arranged by the hospital.

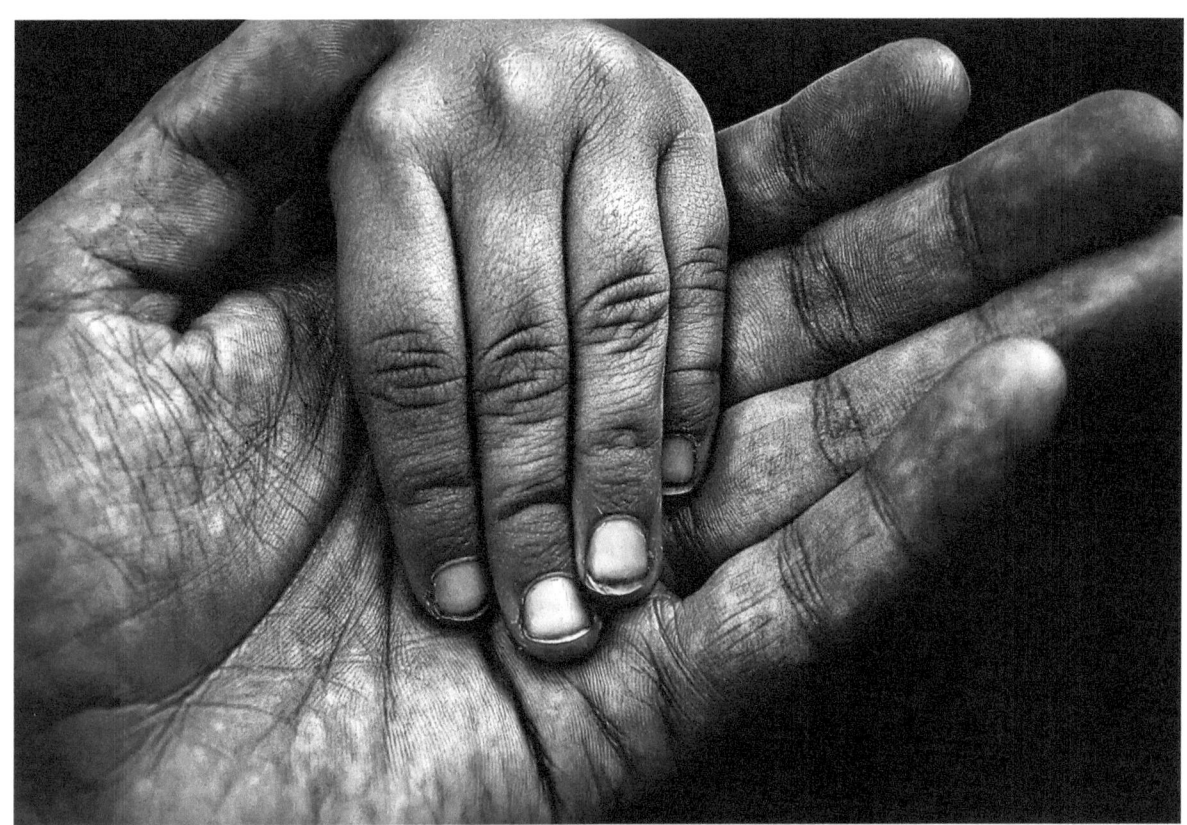

Generations

Almost a million tears I have cried
as I keep asking myself
why did you have to die.
Another birthday slips by
and I wish you were here by my side.

The day you died
part of me died too.
That empty numb feeling
seemed to linger.
Now it's an aching heart
as this pain still threatens to torment me.

Each day is a struggle
as waves of grief wash over me
and tears flow and flow…..

I still yearn to hold you,
to kiss and cuddle you,
to tell you I love you
and will always protect you,
to stroke your face
and smell your hair,
to touch your hands and hold you near,
for our bond has been severed
as mother and son.

"You give but little when you give of your possessions. It is when you give of yourself that you truly give." - Kahlil Gibran

Destination

Now this is my journey
and mine alone...
as the way back is the way forward.

Many people make an impact
in our lives,
and you are one of them.

If I gather all the tears I've wept
and send them up to heaven
please build a stairway back to earth
so that I can feel your presence.
Without hope what have you got?

"Time may heal but the grief never leaves." - anonymous

Tears flowed like rain drops
the day you died.
That pulse of energy, that life force
is now so still.
The air you once breathed
is now not needed
for it's your spirit now
that's taken over.
Luke, you've changed
our lives forever
and for that we can't be bitter.

We anxiously await
your soul to return -
maybe in your brother or sister.
My journey has only just begun.

If the meaning of loss
is measured by heartache
and deep and overwhelming grief,
then maybe we have already
learnt one of life's
most difficult lessons.
If we quantify each step taken
forwards rather than backwards
we will realise that the hardest
part of the journey
is already behind us
It has no boundaries,
the only ingredient
being love.

Port Willunga

So much to give
this selfless act
of a mother's love.

It's a special bond
that develops at conception
and it will always remain
until the very end.

The pain of losing a child
threatens to burn through
the very core of you,
so raw and so powerful
is a mother's love.

"A journey of a thousand miles begins with one small step." - Old Chinese Proverb

"Sometimes our lives don't take the direction we intended; but it then opens up endless possibilities and opportunities that we least expected."
 - anonymous

On the rocks

All of our scars, whether physical
or emotional, tell a unique story.
Grief can't be verbalised with simplicity.
It's measured in tears.
A true friend is there for you to pick up the pieces
when things seem to be falling apart.

Sometimes we struggle with life's uncertainties
and we feel like we have been
literally smashed to pieces…
but out of the depths of despair
I feel your hand guide me
out of this chaos
and towards the light
to a new beginning.

Blackness descends.
I want to let go,
but scared the past
will dictate the future.
It's time to free my soul,
to spread my wings.
The time is right.
It's my destiny.

To rise above all obstacles
takes immense courage,
strength and determination
but the power of the human spirit
can triumph over all.

Take me back
to those early years
when life was simple.
We held no fear.

You were an angel
sent from above,
here to guide us
with your wisdom and love:
immortal in *death* than in *life* itself.
This is not the *end*
but just the *beginning*.

"Every human being is intended to have a character of his own; to be what no others are, and to do what no other can do."
– William Ellery Channing

Port Noarlunga After Dark

Like a wounded soldier in battle
I clamour for refuge.
I feel exposed and under siege
from my past.
I search for a place to seek solace.
My body aches from the stress.
I yearn for sleep but it still eludes me.
This journey seems like torment
as I stumble over familiar ground.
My battle scars a constant
reminder of this grief.

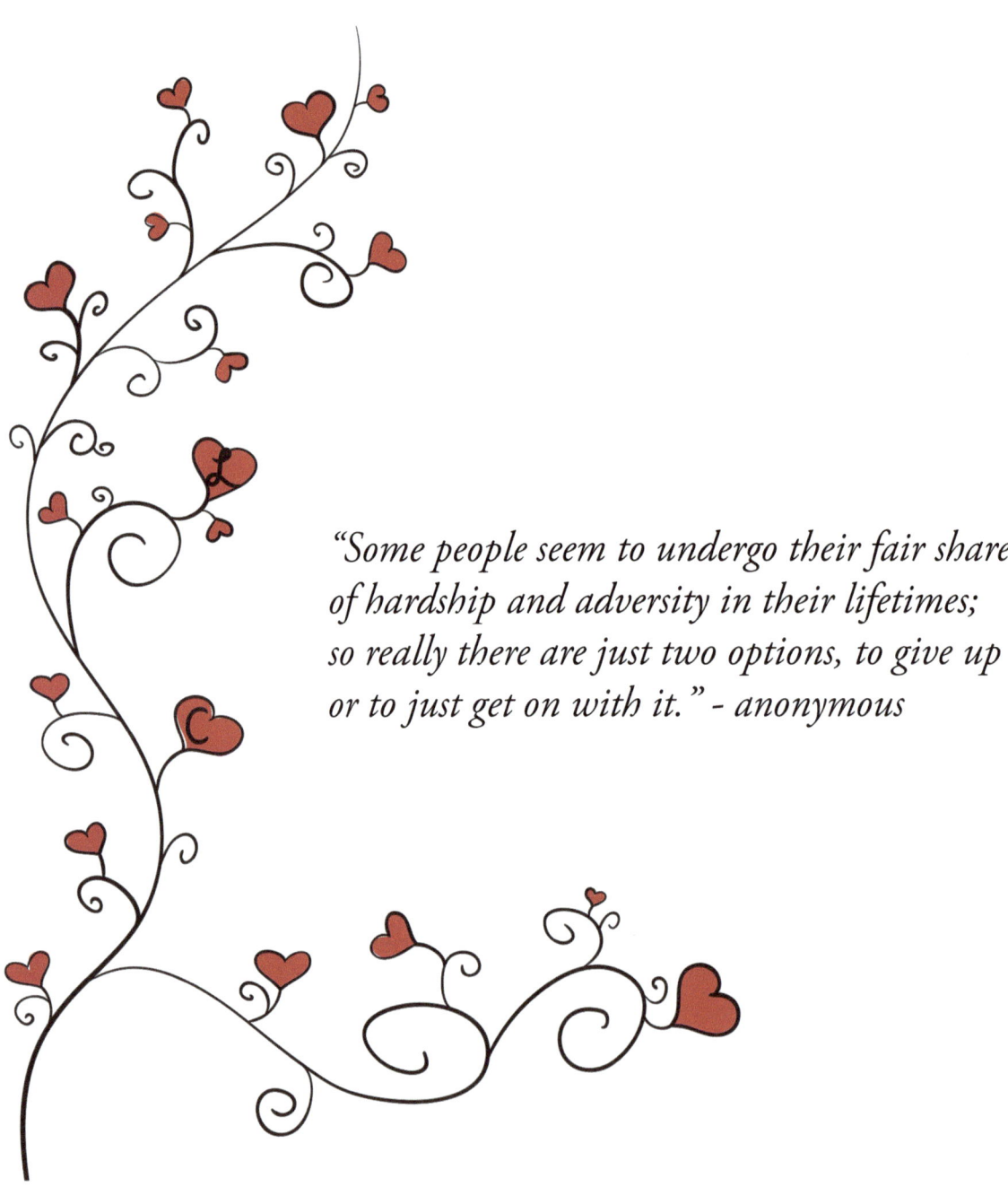

"Some people seem to undergo their fair share of hardship and adversity in their lifetimes; so really there are just two options, to give up or to just get on with it." - anonymous

As we continue through our lives
there are many inspiring people
who touch our souls
in a way we never expected.
One soul enters this earth,
another soul leaves.

As we progress throughout our lives
there are some people who touch us
with their genuine sincerity, concern and support
that at times overwhelms:
but there are so few who move us in ways
that at times almost takes your breath away.

Summer Breeze

You have helped so many parents
come to terms with their loss
and their child's inevitable transition
from that of life to death.
Although many years have passed
and we still continue to recover from our losses
we fondly remember the support and friendship
you gave us during a difficult time.
You have an amazing gift…
but this is our gift to you.

Never underestimate the *power*
of the human *spirit*.
The way *back* is the way forward.
With true clarity, courage and strength
we can overcome any obstacle.

The Journey

Dream not of *who* your are
but of *what* you will become.

Wisdom is indeed gained
by life experiences;
nothing more, nothing less.

Life is overwhelming at times.
You want to revel in all its unique opportunities
but also be equally aware of its uncertainties.
Sometimes we need to experience *death*
before we can truly *live*.

"The turning point in the process of growing up is when you discover the core strength within you that survives all hurt." – Max Lerner

Life is full of challenges
and hardships
but sometimes it is those
occasions that help
define who we are.

Emotions are out of control.
I want to let go
of forever holding on
to the past.
I close my eyes
and open my heart.
It's time to live for now;

reach out,
spread your wings,
open your heart,
dare to sing.

Ethereal-like quality
surpasses all humanity.
Unparalleled clarity
transcends immortality.

It happened one evening.
Another boy we conceived,
but at six months
your soul had decided to leave.

Tragically we never met
in better circumstance,
and we will always wonder
what might have been.

This inner war rages
like so many pages.
Grief is working through stages
but I feel I'm trapped in a cage.

Depth

"The best kind of friend is the one you could sit on a porch with, never saying a word, and walk away feeling like that was the best conversation you've had."- Unknown

"Inner strength and courage is a quality we all possess;but there are some of us that need to draw on this more than others." - anonymous

Port Willunga BW

Whilst my soul is wounded
the enemy has surrounded.
My feet are grounded.
Paralysed with fear,
immobilized it's near.
No longer any fun
it's time to draw the curtain.
I surrender. You've won.

Hope inspires and encourages
but above all creates a feeling of self-belief.

The way you laughed.
The way you walked.
The way you smiled.
The way you talked.

Your blue eyes.
Your blonde hair.
Your large hands.
Skin so fair.

So young.
So wise.
So cute.
Tears in our eyes.

My grief rages.
It's a fire within.
I need to find my courage
so that I can begin.

Waterfall Gully Second Falls

"The meaning of life is to find your gift,
the purpose of life is to give it away." – Joy Golliver

"Life is not measured by the number of breaths we take, but by the moments that take our breath away." – Maya Angelou

About the Author

Jackie lives in Adelaide with her husband of 21 years David, her two daughters Tayla and Mia, and their Lhasa Apso dog Chevy.

Jackie works part-time, as well as running her own business, and writing in her spare time. She contributed a chapter to author Adrienne Ryan's book, A Silent Love, a collection of personal stories based around miscarriage, stillbirth and neonatal death.

The loss of her two sons and her daughter's recent diagnosis prompted this, her first book. A percentage from the purchase price of this book will aid the WCH Foundation, and the Paediatric Palliative Care Service of the WCH, Adelaide SA.

Acknowledgements

This has been incredibly enjoyable to put together, with so much work, but so rewarding on so many levels.

There are so many people to thank, so here goes…

To my husband David: we have weathered the storm, life continues to throw us many challenges… still. But our bond and love for one another, has stayed strong. We have managed to keep our marriage in tact, where many have crumbled under the strain.

To our two girls, Tayla and Mia: you're the reason we have the strength to face each day. Tayla, you have been so brave and so mature over the past nine months. It was a shock when you were diagnosed with a rare neuroendocrine tumour, but we are in this together and we will get through this.

To my mother and father: your love and guidance has been invaluable over the years.

To our many friends: we thank you for your ongoing friendship over the years, and to our immediate families, your love and support has been unwavering. To the many bereaved families, we have been privileged to meet, and to Anne and Neil, we value your friendship.

Andrea, you continue to inspire me, having been through so much already, even with your own health issues, you just get on with it. Thanks for your help with my book.

People come and go in your lifetime, but there are so few that are just amazing, incredible, dedicated and compassionate human beings. I am referring to the staff at the Women's and Children's Hospital, and in particular the Paediatric Palliative Care Service.

Sara, thank you for your support in the early years. After Cody and Luke's deaths, and more recently since Tayla's diagnosis, you are a beautiful caring soul. Thanks for picking up the pieces. At times there are no words to describe the grief, so too there are no words to adequately describe you.

Carina, your support and concern, is also appreciated. You too are a lovely caring and compassionate person.

To the other nurses, doctors and staff of the WCH that we have had the pleasure of knowing, and managed to bump into over the past few months, albeit not as we planned: we are forever indebted for your care of Cody, Luke and more recently Tayla.

To Andy McDermott and the team at Publicious for making this book a reality. Thank you so much.

To an old high school mate, Andrew Williams, who designed the cover for this book, it looks amazing. To Debra Law for the photo shoot, for promotion of the book and website many thanks. Finally to SD Smart for their amazing talents, and who brought some justice to my words, a big thank you.

References

'4 in 3' the Mason Minniss Fund

Mason was diagnosed at ten years of age, with a rare metabolic condition called METACHROMATIC LEUKODYSTROPHY.
MLD is genetic, there is no known cure yet.
Mason is always in our hearts, but we are now a family of 4 in 3 bodies.
In Masons honour we established this fund in 2011, in support of the Women's & Children's Hospital Foundation.
Our fund is supporting families here in Adelaide who are patients of the Paediatric Palliative Care Dept at the Women's & Children's Hospital, Adelaide.
For more information or to make a donation please contact:
Cheryl or Rob Minniss
M: 0417760098
E:masonminnissfund@gmail.com
https://www.facebook.com/4in3theMasonMinnissFund

The Sam Roberts Family Fund

The Sam Roberts Family Fund was established in 2006 following the loss of four year old Sam Roberts. Sam had spent two years living in the Women's & Children's Hospital following his diagnosis of a rare neurological degenerative illness called Niemann Pick Disease Type C, of which there is no cure. There are only 500 cases of this disease in the world.

The Sam Roberts Family Fund proudly supports the Paediatric Palliative Care Service of the Adelaide Women's and Children's Hospital. In particular, The Sam Roberts Family Fund supports families in South Australia who have children battling rare diseases.
The main fund raising campaigns have been centred around the epic "Cycle 4 Sam" bike rides.
For more information or to make a donation please contact:
www.wchfoundation.org.au
www.cycle4sam.com

Heartfelt

Heartfelt is a volunteer organisation of professional photographers from all over Australia dedicated to giving the gift of photographic memories to families that have experienced stillbirths, premature births, or have children with serious and terminal illnesses.
Heartfelt is dedicated to providing this gift to families in a caring, compassionate manner, all services are provided free of charge.
For more information contact:
Ph:1800 583 768
www.heartfelt.org.au

Neuroblastoma Australia

Created by families and friends affected by Neuroblastoma - with support from Children's Cancer Institute of Australia. This non-profit organisation was founded in 2010. Our aim is help raise awareness and

funds for research as well as to offer support to other families affected by Neuroblastoma.
For more information or to make a donation:
Email: neuroblastomaaustraliainc@gmail.com
www.neuroblastoma.org.au

Women's and Children's Hospital Foundation

Since the Foundation was established in 1989, we have supported the Hospital with in excess of $20 million to improve facilities, purchase state-of-the-art equipment and fund life-saving research.
We are committed to ensuring that children and their families have access to the very best in medical care and support services at a time when they need it most.
And that's why we need your help.
Your support will ensure that we can continue to make a difference for South Australian women, babies and children, now and into the future.
Ground Floor
55 King William Road
North Adelaide, SA
T 08 8464 7900
F 08 8464 7999
1800 008 483 (donations)
Postal address
Locked Bag 5
Adelaide SA 5001

Paediatric Palliative Care Service

Our Mission: To serve all children, who have life limiting illnesses, and their families.
Referrals are accepted from health care professionals across the care spectrum.
Families may also access the service without a referral.
Presently the criteria for admission to the Palliative Care Service requires that a child be:
- aged between 0 and 18 years
- diagnosed with a life-limiting illness
- receiving their primary health service in South Australia or Northern Territory.

Women's and Children's Hospital

72 King William Road
North Adelaide
South Australia 5006
Paediatric Palliative Care Service
General Business 8am - 5pm weekdays
Phone (08) 8161 7994
Fax (08) 8161 6631
24 hour on call service, after hours contact 8161 7000 pager 5719
Email cywhs.pallcare@health.sa.gov.au

List of Photographs

Page 0	Generations	SD Smart
Page 2	Luke's Blocks	SD Smart
Page 6	Destination	SD Smart
Page 10	Silver Train (engraving)	SD Smart
Page 12	Port Willunga colour	SD Smart
Page 16	On the rocks	SD Smart
Page 20	Silver Train (front view)	SD Smart
Page 24	Port Noarlunga After Dark	SD Smart
Page 28	Summer Breeze	SD Smart
Page 30	The Journey	SD Smart
Page 34	Silver Train (side view)	SD Smart
Page 40	Depth	SD Smart
Page 44	Port Willunga BW	SD Smart
Page 48	Waterfall Gully Second Falls	SD Smart
Page 53	Jackie & Chevy	Debra Law

www.ingramcontent.com/pod-product-compliance
Lightning Source LLC
Chambersburg PA
CBHW042147290426
44110CB00003B/136